John Shaw
Larry West

VISIONS OF THE WILD
A Photographic Viewpoint

Text by Susan Shaw

BOOK DESIGN: Gijsbert van Frankenhuyzen,
art director, MNR Magazine, Lansing
COLOR SEPARATIONS: The Modern Litho
Corporation, Grand Rapids
PRINTING: The John Henry Company, Lansing
BINDERY: Howard Decker & Son, Grand Rapids
PAPER: 100-pound Number One Vintage
Velvet, The Potlatch Corporation, Northwest
Paper Division, Cloquet, Minnesota
TYPE: Headlines set in Berling. Text in English
Times on the EditWriter 7500
Unless otherwise indicated in Photo Notes, pp.
126-127, all photos are Kodachrome 35mm.
slides, processed by the Kodak Corporation and
owned by the authors.

Visions of the Wild is a publication of Woolly
Bear Productions, a unit of

Ruby-throated hummingbird at orange milkweed.

Preface

Larry West and John and Susan Shaw, the Michigan authors of this book, have all gained national reputations in this growing and fascinating field of outdoor discovery and representation. Their work has appeared in every major publication produced on this continent, including *National Geographic, Audubon, Natural History, National Wildlife,* and many, many others. We are proud to add that our own DNR Magazine, *Michigan Natural Resources,* also has been honored to use many of their photos. Such being the case, it followed that we should soon or late publish a book of their work.

For me personally, and for the staff of the magazine, this book represents both an end point and a beginning. In 1971, the DNR magazine teetered at the edge of collapse. The circulation had never been large and costs were mounting. The question arose: Was there any real need for such a publication? To answer the question, directly, the State Legislature chopped off all appropriations—but allowed the DNR to continue the magazine so long as readers would support it with voluntary subscription dollars.

That gave us pause. Quite abruptly, after 40 years as a tax-supported program of the DNR, the magazine was being cast to a readers' vote. Happily, the book you hold in your hands is the bright, colorful, positive result of that vote—a resounding pledge of confidence from the people of Michigan who have subscribed to the magazine since then, building it to a level of strength where we are now able to begin publication of a corollary series of excellent books about our state. *Visions of The Wild* is the first in this series, a series which we intend to do slowly and well over the next several years.

But let's be clear: No tax money was used to publish this book, no tax money is used to publish the magazine from whose funds it grew, and no tax money will be used to publish the books that stand ahead. Only magazine funds were used to publish this book, and all revenues from the book will return to the magazine fund.

These books and magazines, we know now, are virtually *required* by the thousands of our readers who delight in the history, the visual beauty, and the outdoor chronicles of this colorful region. The magazine/book fund has thus become a no-profit state government experiment that does its work for the people who have paid to build it. It's their fund and these are their books and magazines, and we who have the luck to work in these vineyards are acutely aware of the outdoor values such publications represent. Those values are a growing and proud Michigan tradition, and we in the DNR are proud to be part of it.

Russell McKee, editor
Michigan Natural Resources Magazine
Lansing, November, 1980.

VISIONS OF THE WILD

Canada goose at sunrise.

The essence of this book is the experience of the natural landscape. There are times throughout the seasons when landscapes commonly beheld as ordinary become transformed and remade, changing from the mundane to the exotic. These transformations are the result of many factors: the turn of the season, seldom observed times of day, weather, patterns of light and shadow, and chance encounters with other living creatures. But the most important factor is the participant/observer. Without the proper attitude, a wideness of vision, a truly fresh beginner's enthusiasm, no transformation takes place.

We are photographers who have lived with and studied the natural world. We have endeavored to capture photographically the transcendental nature of time and space. There is something tangible in these wild moments that film can portray. Both of us have spent many years afield, walking, waiting, sometimes for hours, looking, until a photograph is discovered. It can happen anywhere, from a suburban backyard to a wilderness watercourse. This then is how the pictures for this book came to be; they are a product of a continuing love affair with light, seasons, meadows, and woodlots—the outdoors. Light in its infinite manifestations, creatures large and small. These photographs are a memory, a knowing of the world through two sets of eyes, a vision of the wild.

The Great Debate

I am lying on the sloping bank in the tall dry grass of autumn in the warmth of the afternoon sun. The grasses sway above me. The two serious photographers have travelled on down this hill. They've set up in the little lake below, right in the lake. They have hip boots, waders, and a ladder. Yes, a *ladder*. I'm not sure what they're up to. I suspect they're looking for a new perspective. They're always looking for something. The exact point at which they leave most of the rest of us behind is that they always *see* something.

Now a car pulls up on the bridge just above me. People get out. They can't see me. They can see the two below, in the lake, with the ladder. The great debate begins. I've heard this so many times I want to laugh, but I don't want to give myself away. Although I would love to rise up from the grasses with this little butterfly riding like a small falcon on one arm and answer all their questions in a true oracular fashion. But I can't rise up out of the grasses with a butterfly on my arm because I've lost my identity, or found a larger one. I'm just warm earth now myself. To be unpoetic, I'm half asleep. It doesn't matter. I know this by heart.

"What are those two fellas doing?"

"I don't know. Beats me. Maybe they're fishing."

"They've got a ladder though. I mean what have they got a ladder for?"

"Why, I don't know. They could be fishing."

"I know. See that thing, whaddya call it?"

"A tripod. They're taking pictures. But what are they taking pictures of?"

"I expect the fall color."

"Down there in the lake?"

"Well, maybe there's a moose or beaver or something."

"I don't see anything. Sure wish I knew what they need that ladder for."

"Something must be down there."

"Nah. Nothing's down there. Let's move on."

Yes, something is down there. Maybe I can't answer all the questions. Maybe I don't know exactly what they're doing, but I do know what they see. It is something quite alive and tangible to them, something mysterious. The ladder isn't mysterious, it's just equipment for height, a short aerial view. Equipment is always secondary. Seeing is primary. There is something moving mysteriously across the surface of the water. It's not a fish. It's not even a colored leaf floating by. They're after what they're always after. This time they happen to be chasing it around on the water. They've abandoned the ladder. They are wading around. I can hear them.

"Look at that. Do you see that? Let's get it. We've got to get that."

"I've got it. Isn't that sweet? Boy, did you get it? I sure hope I got that."

They sound like children, these two serious photographers. See it. Hold it. Catch it. That's the game. What is it? What is this mysterious thing that they see that few others can? It's just the sunlight. That's all it is. Just the light.

At left, lily pads at sunrise.

Above, female cardinal.

At left, raindrops on spotted touch-me-not.

Above, withered oak leaf on forest floor.

The Alchemy of Light

The first thing, the best thing, is to be there, alone, at the dawning in the dew, waiting for the light. Maybe now and then you can bring one other person with you. You can't bring a crowd with you—crowd of people, crowd of thoughts, crowd of expectations, crowd of equipment, crowd of candy bars or beer cans, or appetites or egos. Leave them all behind. In order to see clearly you have to be alone.

Alone. First creature on a new planet. Morning is new, each one. Every afternoon-ordinary-thing looks unfamiliar now. Afternoon hasn't been created yet. Good, I'm slowing down. Slowing, slowing, losing time, drifting, gliding like a lark into the morning sky. Red light, blue light, waves of light. The whole sky is tossing like the ocean. Slow it down. Stop it. Capture it in a net. Draw it in. Bring that sky down here. A rectangular net, that's what this camera is sometimes—a way to bring things in.

Dragonfly, heavy with dew, unable to fly, I don't want to touch you, net you, or change you in any way. Listen, we can both be alone on this planet. I'll just stand a few feet off here and view you. Send my eye flying over there with this magic black box. I don't have to slow you down, dragonfly; you've already stopped. Just let me gaze into your eyes. They are hypnotic. Irridescent hexagons. Irridescent hexagons. More irridescent hexagons. I can't take too much of this. The light is really bounding around in there and on your wings it's dancing, and now some kind of explosion is going on in your eyes—ah, yes, sunrise.

Foggy sunrise, bur oak.

On the following pages: 14-15, winter field; 16-17, hawkweed meadow; 18-19, midwinter moon rise.

At left, shaft of light in Tahquamenon Forest.
Above, dewy sheet web over British soldier lichens.

The light falls from the sky now. Light is falling everywhere, spreading through the woods, touching everything. I am looking everywhere, seeing everything. Seeing only one thing: the light. I have to get it while it's down here on the earth. It's weaving through the maple branches. It soothes my cold hands. It's awakening the dragonfly. It's dripping from the plants with the dew. It's flowing down the sides of the trees. It's burning the dew off this spider web. I can almost see it smoking. No, that's steam off the grasses. There's the 200th picture I missed this morning.

At left, stream in Nethercut Woods.

Above, raindrop covered sheet web.

I have to catch
something here.
Have to focus in
on one thing.

left, twig with hoar frost.

Above, raindrops on feather.

The first thing, the best thing, is to be there, alone, at the dawning, waiting for the light.

Forest fog at sunrise.

akeshore in fog,

utumn tamaracks encircling bog eye.

es in fog.

Alchemy... the
right light on the
right leaf in the
right season
renders gold.

At left, oak leaf melting up through ice.
Above, foxtail grass at sunset.

Above, green heron at daybreak.

At right, cattails early August morni

The Spell of Water

So this is what you see when the light comes: a dewdrop world. Everything transient: changing, thawing, freezing, melting, flowing. Drip-drop, drip-drop, raindrops down a windowpane.

A dewdrop world it is,
a dewdrop world it remains.
And yet... and yet...
Issa

The thing that old ironic Issa knew is that sadness has something to do with seeking permanence. Enter the photographer, taking his pictures, seeming to be a cold observer but being ironically human, seeking his permanence. And what do the pictures reveal? There is no permanence. The natural world is in flux. Everything is changing: swirling pools, roaring falls, clouds, snow, raindrops. It's all just water and wind and weather. We're not a part of this, are we? We have solid facts, words, ideas, philosophies, ideologies—permanence. Drip-drop, drip-drop, drip-drop, the rains of the centuries wash them all away. Let's not identify with a duck or a reed or a frog or a tree. Let's not drift or flow like water to the sea. Let's stay in one place and pretend to permanence. I mean, even spiders have their webs, although it's true they're spun anew each morning.

Dewy spider webs,
field after field,
catching the sunrise.
Mainone

Photographs are revelations, sometimes painful, sometimes beautiful. It's not easy being human. They say art isn't reality and photography isn't an art, but sometimes it's hard to tell the reeds from the reflections. Well, then, the question is what is it? It

seeing, searching, finding only
that everything is changing,
finding a larger identity.

Morning fog
becoming this,
becoming that.
            Mainone

Pollen covered raindrop on web strand.

On the following pages: 36-37, Lake Michigan beach, late
afternoon; 38-39, reeds in water, summer twilight; 40-41,
frost covered plants and frozen pond.

Above, pale corydalis.
At right, dew covered dragonfly on grass head.

"What are you looking for?"

"Something that isn't blowing around. Something that doesn't fly away. Something that doesn't move an inch, but it's beautiful, if you get my drift."

" Let's see. This isn't that hard.... Wet rocks!"

"Hey! They do move pretty slowly, don't they. Maybe there'll be fewer black flies and mosquitoes out in the open stream. Maybe I'll just wade or listen to the stream."

"You don't have to photograph."

"I know. What a relief! You do though, don't you, John?"

"I want to. I can't sit there and listen to the stream for an hour like you do. I'm not contemplative."

"Oh sure, I know. You're hyperactive, except when you're crouched over the same flower or insect for, oh say, two or three days. It's a kind of Zen, that's what it is."

"It was only thirty minutes tops."

"Several years elapsed there, John. We were in a time warp. There wasn't any time for you but shutter speed, the speed of light."

At left, dewy web section.
Above, twin orb webs on dead sapling.

Above, green frog.

At right, arrowhead and foggy summer sunr

"Where's West? I thought e was photographing the ream."

"He's lost, John. West and I re always lost. Some people refer to be that way."

"There he is, conversing with ogs again."

"He appears to be a frog. Vhat have you got, West?"

"I don't know, but it's rare. 's one of a kind. I've shot a hole roll of film on this frog."

Shaw, shrugging: "It's a ecent frog."

At left, dragonfly emerging from nymphal skin.

Above, western chorus frog singing.

So this is what
you see when the
light comes:
a dewdrop world.

Spring pond.

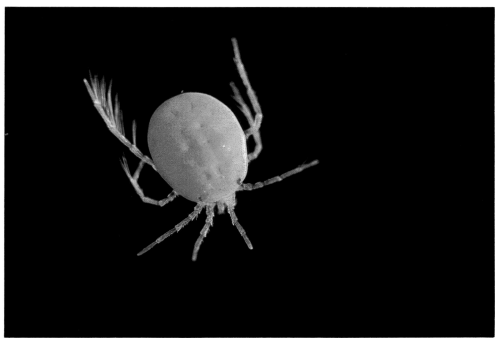

Hydracarina mite.

naria, sp.

Copepod.

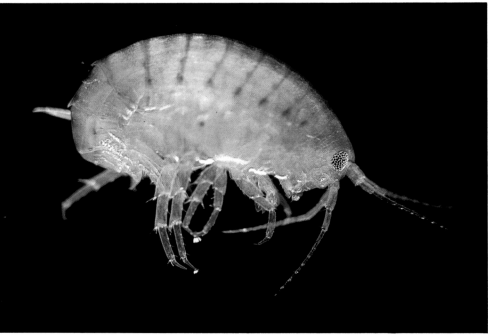

Amphipod gammarus, sp.

t left, Grand Sable Falls, autumn.   Above, dew covered arcadian hairstreak.

It is seeing and
searching, finding
at last that
everything
keeps changing.

Wolf Creek in midwinter.

Ice cave on Grand Island.

One waits also for
miracles: things
never seen before,
or seen only once.

Above, summer frost on star thistle.

At right, frosted black oak and blueberry, Octobe

Woodlot and wet snow.

Skunk tracks and sedges.

Oak trunks and shadows.

Hour to hour,
season to season,
one seeks the
light, searching,
waiting,
slowing down.

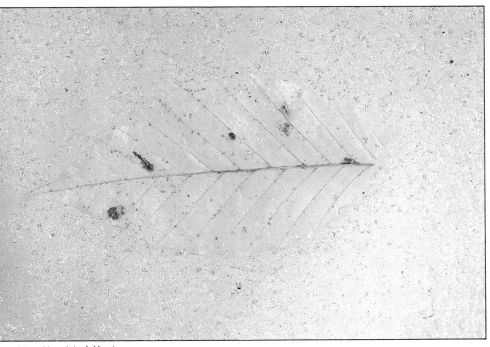

verwintered beech leaf, March.

Let's not drift or
flow like water to
the sea. Let's stay
in one place
and pretend to
permanence.

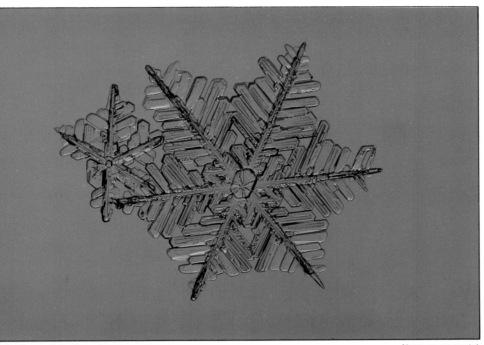

left, Wagner Falls, December.

Above, snow crystal.

Dewdrops.

We have solid
facts, ideas,
ideologies—
permanence.
Drip-drop,
the rains of the
centuries wash
them all away.

ndrop.

Visions of Life

When I go out, not only looking but looking *for* something, then the search becomes a hunt. Study the tracks and traces. Clues are everywhere. Traces of life, and death, large and small. Unsolved mysteries. Vision becomes acute. The slightest movement is perceived. The senses are heightened. Sounds and smells and even feelings are important, such as "I feel that I am being watched," an important feeling to have at all times in the woods because at all times it's true. Knowing that, you just have to locate the eyes of the watcher. Maybe above you, owl's eyes, maybe on your shoulder a fly, maybe from beneath a green leaf a spider, maybe the golden-ringed eyes of frogs, maybe high-above hawks eyes, in the shade doe's eyes, eyes of a fawn, in the shadows coyote's eyes and... have I lost the thought? Good. To hunt best I have to lose thought; that is, to stop thinking like a human.

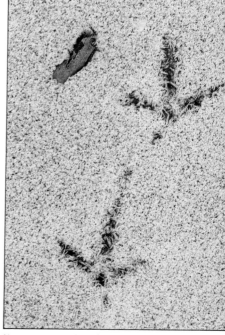

Above, grouse tracks in frost.   At right, tracks and peta

left, yellow-bellied sapsucker.   Above, western meadowlark.

I'm after deer. This isn't me thinking, I've cut that out. I'm not human.

*Fleeter be than dappled dreams
the swift sweet deer
the red rare deer.*

That's not me, that's e.e. cummings. I'm running, running. On a deertrail. Winter. Late afternoon. To the stream! They'll be there at the thawing stream, pawing and snorting. Their breath clouds of steam. Snowstars shining in their fur. Bird call. A few flute notes tinkling in the air, more delicate

Melting snow and reflections.

han windchimes. Sound of rushed sweet fern, red osiers, a blurring red and brown and black, the trunks of trees fly past. Snow melting, scent of mud and moss, dank and sweet. What's that? A small movement in the brush. Twitch of an ear. Rabbit's eye. Now he's running, running. Now I hear them.

Softer be they than slippered sleep
the lean lithe deer
the fleet flown deer.

Their hooves are delicately wending, single filing down to the stream. From the brush across the stream I watch them. I stand slowly, slowly coming out of my crouch. A buck snorts and paws. "We are the people of these woods," their eyes tell me. "Here we belong. You do not. It's getting dark. Go back to your home with its yellow window light. We need only the light of the moon."

They run. Not far. They are watching me from the brush. The way deer regard me always makes me feel like a wraith. Why must they startle like that? Then that curious accusing stare. Then flight, but not far. The woods do belong to them, I agree. It was a long winter.

Paler be they than daunting death
the sleek, slim deer
the tall tense deer.

In that glance I know something. With or without a gun, with or without a camera, I am always to them the hunter. It's getting darker. The moon rises. A barred owl calls. Ancient hunting sounds fill the woods, and darkness is coming. Why do I feel hunted? We are a people of the light, a technological people. We have pushed the darkness far, far away into the hills and forests. Why do we return?

Spinning with the
infinity of the
galaxies is the
small sharp death
of an insect stilled
in the spider's
spinning.

At left, insects trapped in orb web.
Above, feathers and blood spot.

Above, cinnamon fern, autumn.   At right, cinnamon fern, midsumme

The lights and
hues of each
season, as each
time of day, are
singularly distinct
to that time and
season.

At left, fly amanita mushroom.
Above, autumn landscape.

Above, European skipper on grass pink orchid.
At right, pearly eye.

Goldenrod field.

There is much
seeking, seeing,
searching; and in
the time it takes
a shutter to
click, there is
the finding.

sture rose amidst prairie sedges.

Spotted coralroot orchid.

Long-eared owl.

"I feel that I am being watched," an important feeling to have at all times in the woods because at all times it's true.

emale mallard duck.

American toad.

obber fly.

Sound of crushed
sweet fern.
What's that?
A small
movement
in the brush.
Twitch of an ear.

left, Eastern chipmunk.

Above, bobcat.

Travels in Time

To photographers the seasons look much like the light of day: spring is blue and fresh and gentle as morning; summer, green and golden and warm as afternoon; fall is twilight, dusky, cool, red and blue; winter lies white and crystalline, clear and starry as night. This is all the time there is. There is no nine to five, five days a week. No Ides of March. However, there are important dates.

The full moon, for instance. An important date for which one must not be too late or too early. One must also appear on time for the opening night of a great symphony—the voices of the spring frogs. And there is the first dance of a butterfly in flight. The graceful struggle from the chrysalis. The leap to the sky and the gentle descent light-footed upon the petals of a flower.

er swallowtail in flight.

Intuition can lead one to the right place at the right time: How to know which tree trunk to single out in any given forest; On which tree trunk or in which swaying branches will one find the travellers—squirrel, porcupine, bobcat, the hunting hawks.

At left, gray squirrel. Above, marsh hawk feeding on snake.

Empty snail shell on seedling.

Aged bloom of large flowered trillium.

Timing is everything and time means nothing. How much time will it take to find the most beautiful meadow out of all the meadows on this planet. Perhaps a lifetime. Perhaps they are all the most beautiful. An expert's knowledge of the natural world is necessary to find the right butterfly on its favorite flower in one small wet meadow in the right season. The larva of the Baltimore checker feeds only on turtlehead. To find the chrysalid one must know the plant called turtlehead.

On the following pages: 98-99, sunrise over low meadow. 100-101, field of bergamot.

ae of Baltimore checker butterfly.

Mammatocumulus clouds.

nterberry holly.

Photographers travel in the sky as well. Always they watch the weather, the clouds, the winds, the light from sunrise to sunset. They do not lose patience but will return again to haunt a favorite woods or bog or beach.

The photographs achieved may be timeless. A hundred centuries ago a tulip tree leaf or a witch hazel bloom looked the same as now, and in the future if a species is lost the photo will journey back to the green past. Will the future be green too? Or will the world be as gray as concrete sidewalks? Photographers struggle to preserve the earth as well as their own images of beauty.

Above, aspen leaves, early morning.
At right, fallen leaf of tulip tree.

There is much seeking, seeing, searching, and in the time it takes a shutter to click, there is the finding. A moment of knowing. Something is revealed. Some essence distilled. With the speed and illumination of a lightning flash, past and future are made one in the present moment. We are given a vision.

Pussy willow.

Autumn frost on witch hazel blossoms.

left, bowl and doily web on blueberry.   Above, fall color and approaching storm.

No single death is small. All life is large and worth sharing, yet death is a small thing in this universe. Births and deaths occur each moment. Stars are born and others die. Spinning with the infinity of the galaxies is the small sharp death of an insect stilled in the spider's spinning. The earth's soil receives its creatures and gives back new life and growth. The skeleton of a bird is much like a man's. The one can fly, the other dream.

Fall is a death and the woods feel it. A storm approaches. Quivering, the deer flee through the red sumac. The scent is heavy and damp with dust and dry leaves. In the wild storm light, the animals awaken out of sleep. The ground trembles. The wind is a dance of trees. Aspen leaves shoot off like sparks. In the morning most of the leaves will lie on the golden ground. The photographer knows this. He backs off. He waits for just the right storm glimmerings. The right heaviness of gray in the sky. The one moment of the wind's dying down. The precise red-gold illumination. The photographer feels the sharp cold, the winter wind that's come too soon. Even a single leaf sailing down may be sad and beautiful. There will be a new spring, new green leaves, and yet, and yet...

A still moment comes. A picture is taken—another small death. The photographer knows this, that he must capture his subject and yet it must be alive, as close to life as dream is to reality. What is a good photograph? It is somehow alive with echoings of light, and color. The dampness of the air must be felt in it. A sense of movement must be there, of a breeze just stilled, a raindrop just fallen, prey just taken. A flower trembles into bloom, opening and softly falling to the arth, an exquisite act which we all "dying." All this must be rdered within the frame with ne mathematician's precision nd the artist's keen sight nd intuition.

A vision is given, not only to ne senses, but to the eyes of the iind. Imagination must be eized. Drama, or stark implicity, or subtle delicacy, it's ll power. A blade of grass ways softly, is stilled in the hoto, and yet sways again. The cent of fall ferns, the sound of single piping spring peeper, or f a rushing waterfall, once nown is not easily forgotten. he velvet ruffling of a grouse's

feathers, the nervous movement of a chipmunk, the curious proud lifting of the proud heads of the deer—all this is worth remembering.

But is it just a memory? Past and future come together in the best photographs. In the vision of the moment something new is learned about time: there isn't any. Time is a human invention just like the camera. Both serve a purpose. We like to order our universe and to perceive order; this is history. Take light and water and swirl them in the crucible of time and we have life; this is alchemy.

Above, young spruce growing from pine stump.
On the following pages: 112-113, staghorn sumac.

Young leaves of swamp white oak.

A sense of
movement must
be there, of a
breeze just stilled,
a raindrop just
fallen.

ring woods in light rain.

left, foxtail grass.

Above, rain covered oak leaves.

The one moment of the wind's dying down. The precise red-gold illumination.

Above, maple and hemlock seedlings.
At right, branch of autumn tamarack.

Grouse incubating.

Past and future
come together.
In the vision of
the moment
something new is
learned about
time.

Aged cardinal.

No single death is small. All life is large and worth sharing, yet death is a small thing in this universe.

Above, bird skull in pine needles.
At right, withered bullhead-lily.

200mm with reversed 105mm as supplementary, 10 sec. f32, k25

65. Raindrop.
200mm with reversed 105 mm as supplementary, 10 sec. f32, k25

66. Grouse tracks in frost.
105mm, 1/2 sec. f11, k25

67. Tracks and petals.
105mm, 1/15 sec. f11, k25

68. Yellow-bellied sapsucker.
300mm, 1/60 sec. f11, k25, electronic flash.

69. Western meadowlark.
400mm. 1/250 sec. f5.6, k25

70. Melting snow and reflections.
200mm, 1/2 sec. f11, k25

72. Insects trapped in orb web.
105mm, 1/60 sec. f11-16, k25, electronic flash

73. Feathers and blood spot.
105mm, 1/30 sec. f16, k25

74. Mossy deer skull.
105mm, 10 sec. f11, k25

75. White-tailed deer.
300mm, 1/30 sec. f4.5, k25, E200

76. Cinnamon fern, autumn.
105mm, 1/2 sec. f16, k25

77. Cinnamon fern, midsummer.
105mm, 1/4 sec. f16, k25

78. Joe-pye weed meadow.
105mm, 1 sec. f16, k25

79. Maple trees in fog.
50mm, 1/15 sec. f11, k25

80. Porcupine.
200mm, 1/15 sec. f11, k25

81. Great crested flycatcher.
300mm, 1/30 sec. f11, k25

82. Fly amanita mushroom.
105mm, 1/2 sec. f11, k25

83. Autumn landscape.
24 mm, 1/4 sec. f16, k25

84. European skipper on grass pink orchid.

105mm, 1/30 sec. f8, k25

85. Pearly eye.
200mm, 1 sec. f11, k25

86. Goldenrod field.
50mm, 1/2 sec. f16, k25

87. Pasture rose amidst prairie sedges.
105mm, 1/4 sec. f16, k25

88. (Top) Spotted coralroot orchid.
105mm, 1/60 sec. f16, k25, electronic flash

88. (Bottom) Long-eared owl.
500mm, 1/30 sec. f8, k25

89. (Right-top) American toad.
105mm, 1/60 sec. f11-16, k25, electronic flash

89. (Left-top) Female mallard duck.
400mm, 1/250 sec. f5.6, k25

89. (Bottom) Robber fly.
200mm with reversed 105mm as supplementary, 1/60 sec. f22-32, k25, electronic flash

90. Eastern chipmunk.
300mm, 1/60 sec. f11, k25, electronic flash

91. Bobcat.
105mm, 1/30 sec. f4, k25

93. Tiger swallowtail in flight.
200mm, 1/15 sec, f11, k25

94. Gray squirrel.
300mm, 1/125 sec. f8, k25

95. Marsh hawk feeding on snake.
300mm, 1/30 sec. f8, k25

96. (Left) Empty snail shell on seedling. 105mm, 1/2 sec. f11, k25

96. (Right) Aged bloom of large flowered trillium.
105mm, 10 sec. f11, k25

97. Pupae of Baltimore checker butterfly.
105mm, 1 sec. f11, k25

98-99. Sunrise over low meadow.
200mm, 1/4 sec. f11, k25

100-101. Field of bergamot.

105mm, 1/15 sec. f16, k25

102. Mammatocumulus clouds.
24mm, 1/125 sec. f8, k25

103. Winterberry holly.
35mm, 1 sec. f16, k25

104. Aspen leaves, early morning.
200mm, 1/15 sec. f11, k25

105. Fallen leaf of tulip tree.
105mm, 1/2 sec. f11, k25

106. Pussy willow.
200mm, 1 sec. f11, k25

107. Autumn frost on witch hazel blossoms.
105mm, 1/2 sec. f16, k25

108. Bowl and doily web on blueberry.
100mm, 1/8 sec. f11, k25

109. Fall color and approaching storm.
50mm, 1/30 sec. f16, k25

111. Young spruce growing from pine stump.
200mm, 1/2 sec. f11, k25

112-113. Staghorn sumac.
105mm, 1 sec. f11, k25

114. Young leaves of swamp white oak.
200mm, 1 sec. f16, k25

115. Spring woods in light rain.
105mm, 1 sec. f16, k25

116. Foxtail grass.
105mm, 1 sec. f16, k25

117. Rain covered oak leaves.
105mm, 1/2 sec. f22, k25

118. Maple and hemlock seedlings.
105mm, 1/2 sec. f16, k25

119. Branch of autumn tamarack.
105mm, 1 sec. f8, k25

120. Grouse incubating.
400mm, 20 sec. f16, k25

121. Aged cardinal.
600mm, 1/250 sec. f8, k64

122. Bird skull in pine needles.
105mm, 1 sec. f16, k25

123. Withered bullhead-lily.
105mm, 1 sec. f16, k25